Spirit HORSES

PHOTOGRAPHS BY TONY STROMBERG

FOREWORD BY LINDA KOHANOV

NEW WORLD LIBRARY
NOVATO, CALIFORNIA

New World Library
14 Pamaron Way
Novato, CA 94949

Cover and interior design by Mary Ann Casler
Front cover image of Sacajawea from La Estancia Alegre Peruvian Paso Horses
Library of Congress Cataloging-in-Publication Data

First printing, November 2005
ISBN-13 978-1-57731-499-8
ISBN 1-57731-499-9
Printed in China
Distributed to the trade by Publishers Group West

10 9 8 7 6 5 4 3

This book is for Claudia,

and for the horses,
who for centuries
have served and taught us
without expectation for
anything in return.

They deserve to be loved,
respected, and honored.
Let them run free again.
Let them no longer be
faithful beasts, but let us
embrace them as the true
friends and profound
teachers they are
and have always been.

FOREWORD

The horses are gathering, reminding us of a truth that can never be corralled by words. The white mare on the horizon only appears to stand alone. Sentinel of a much larger herd, she embodies a disarming paradox of power and vulnerability, intelligence and innocence. Sometimes she outruns predators; sometimes she outwits them. And then she goes back to grazing. Trust flows through her veins. The world, after all, is a salad to her.

Who knows where the individual ends and the group mind begins? The edges blur in stampedes synchronized through fields of shared emotion. Fear shoots through the herd like lightning, but so does ecstasy. Pleasure flows across the collective psyche like the scent of wild honeysuckle, and peace brushes softly against the face with the swish of a tail. Watch two stallions approach each other, however, and you'll feel the force of personalities ready to explode on impact.

Even staring out of a well-kept stall, the horse is freedom's promise. The sunset may reflect off barbed wire, but domesticated horses remain connected to a paradise they can never lose. If only we would step out of the saddle, turn them loose, and follow them bravely, diligently, humbly, to the oasis at the end of that dusty trail....

The civilized spirit rejoices at the sight of a magnificent stallion racing across the plains with his mares and foals. In this eternally powerful image, we glimpse the possibility that freedom doesn't mean abandoning family, becoming a lone wolf to escape the mundane realities of the society that domesticated us. Rather, we too might reclaim our wildness, our trust in the universe, our understanding of what it means to collaborate with nature rather than dominate her, if only we had the nerve to go feral.

Mustangs are the descendents of domesticated horses, imported from Europe, who escaped a bloody battle or simply wandered away from a conquistador's camp one night. Occasionally, someone uses this as an excuse to round them up and exterminate them. This person invariably marvels at the public outcry. We don't, after all, consider feral cats, dogs, or parakeets symbols of the American West. But no domesticated species seems to *thrive* in the absence of human stewardship like the horse, and for this reason alone we must protect the right of some herds to exist on their own terms if we want to tap the wisdom we ourselves lost so long ago.

Centuries of war, competition, and land exploitation have left us feeling empty and unfulfilled, not to mention skeptical of our own long-term survival. It is time to humbly learn from this nonpredatory species with its gift for flowing effortlessly between what is civilized and what is wild. Left to their own devices, horses prove more resilient, adaptable, and compassionate than most people imagine. Feral herds, for instance, do not form strict pecking orders. The stallion may defer to the alpha mare, and even she may not always be in charge. In a crisis, it's sometimes the mild-mannered horse standing peacefully in the shade, the one who would never presume to drink first from the watering hole, who confidently leads everyone to safety. Two stallions occasionally will share a band of mares, and some males gather mates of a specific color, much like certain men show a preference for blonds or redheads.

Females are simply more empowered and males gentler than our treasured horse myths have led us to believe, and here is where we stand to learn the most from their feral family life. In her documentary *Cloud: Wild Stallion of the Rockies*, Ginger Kathrens followed a striking pale horse through his life, finding that when he successfully wooed his first mare, it didn't happen "in a furious clash of teeth and hooves, but in a moment of stillness." The mare had given birth to a sickly foal, the filmmaker reveals, "and when she stayed with her newborn rather than rejoining her band, Cloud found her and stood quietly by her side." When the foal died, Cloud stayed with the mare and her yearling son by another stallion. After seasons of rough play in bachelor bands, and serious fights with harem stallions that left him scarred and temporarily lame, it was ultimately an act of compassion that won Cloud the privilege of starting his own family.

The horse, long a symbol of power and freedom, is more specifically a teacher of *nonpredatory* power and freedom *through relationship*. Those adventurous souls who follow the ways of horses almost can't help becoming more balanced, confident, and peaceful, more open to the beauty and sacredness of life. Moving among the herds, these people recover a heightened sensitivity to the environment and to others — and, most importantly, the courage to embrace that sensitivity.

Tony Stromberg has taken this journey, and his photos reveal nuances beyond words. Through a masterful blend of realism and mysticism, his images give us an intimate glimpse into the secret life of horses. Spend some time alone with this book, and you'll hear the wind blowing, smell the dry air, feel the sun warming your face, taste the dust flying, feel it stinging the skin. And you'll begin to know the wonder of what it means to leave the city life behind and follow the horses, wandering ever more confidently into the wilderness, developing a hide sensitive yet thick enough to weather the storms of your own forgotten dreams.

Linda Kohanov,
author of *The Tao of Equus* and *Riding between the Worlds*
Spring 2005

INTRODUCTION

"Let the beauty we love be what we do." — RUMI

Like most people, I began my life and career with a vision of success defined by the culture in which I was born. This vision was based on competition. A good income and a nice home were the ultimate goal. Following this path innocently, but diligently, I found my way into a successful career as a commercial photographer in the fast-paced advertising world of San Francisco. Although I won some prestigious awards for my work and felt like I was riding the crest of a wave, at the same time I couldn't ignore a deeper sense of emptiness a feeling that the world I lived in was out of balance. As I made room for this whisper calling to me under the surface, my need for outer approval began to diminish.

At the time, I didn't realize the impact a friend's invitation to get involved with horses would have on my life. I started spending more time in nature, away from the polished concrete of downtown, and reconnecting with the part of me that had always found solace and comfort in the presence of both animals and the wild. I had been forgetting, and ignoring, this part of life for far too long.

I finally left the false security and structure of the corporate world to embrace a path that nurtured, rather than negated, life and spirit. My move to New Mexico just before the turn of the millennium satisfied my soul's increasing need for stillness and space, and provided plenty of opportunity to listen more deeply, through my photography, to what horses had to tell me. Like the old saying, "when the student is ready, the teacher will appear," horses rather quickly became a permanent part of my life and work. This was also the faint beginning of a new belief that I could do what I loved and what nourished me, rather than what didn't.

Through the unfolding of this book, I came to learn that horses remind us of valuable truths that are beginning to fade in our culture. These include collaboration instead of dominance. Honesty and authenticity versus manipulation and falseness. Presence versus distraction. Trust and leadership. Harmony, community, and the plain truth that we are all connected.

Horses exemplify something to me that everyone longs for on some deeper, archetypal level. After years of very precise

and tightly directed advertising photography, I found a layer deep inside myself that literally craved something wild, something unrestrained, something raw and without boundaries — something out of control.

We as a culture are sorely out of connection with the natural world around us. Many of us long for it, but we simultaneously fear it, because it has become so unfamiliar. I hope the images in this book, and the spirit of the horse they represent, can help rekindle some of this wildness in readers open to receiving it.

When the seed for this book slowly began to germinate, I had grandiose plans. I felt I had a lot to share about our world's precarious lack of balance. But I soon realized I didn't have to say anything at all, at least not in writing. I realized the horses were *already saying it*, simply through their presence, and that my role, so to speak, was to share what I have seen in the language that makes the most sense to me. This book is a visual book. It draws its strength from the very simplicity and grace that horses *live*. To complement this visual simplicity, I've included short, select quotations from the writings of great minds that present important truths about our connection with these and other animals.

Horses are not complicated, but neither are the deepest spiritual truths. It is man who makes the simplest truth complicated. My hope is that whoever finds this book can absorb the message of these magnificent teachers through seeing and feeling, rather than through the intellect. It is also my hope that these images might reawaken a place inside us that resonates with that deeper, more ancient truth that horses embody and bring to our world. And that maybe we are ready to listen.

Tony Stromberg
Spring 2005

In the beginning of all things, wisdom and knowledge were with the animals, for Tirawa, the One Above, did not speak to man. He sent certain animals to tell men that he showed himself through the beasts, and that from them, and from the stars and the moon, man should learn.

— PAWNEE CHIEF LEKOTA-LESA

Not to hurt our humble brethren is our first duty
to them, but to stop there is not enough. We
have a higher mission — to be of service to them
wherever they require it.

— SAINT FRANCIS OF ASSISI

We must see these creatures who live in our midst not as a replacement for their wild cousins but as a connection to the wild. Let us never forget our roots. . . . If we ever cut ourselves apart from the wilderness from whence we arose, we will no longer be human.

— DON HAMILTON, DVM

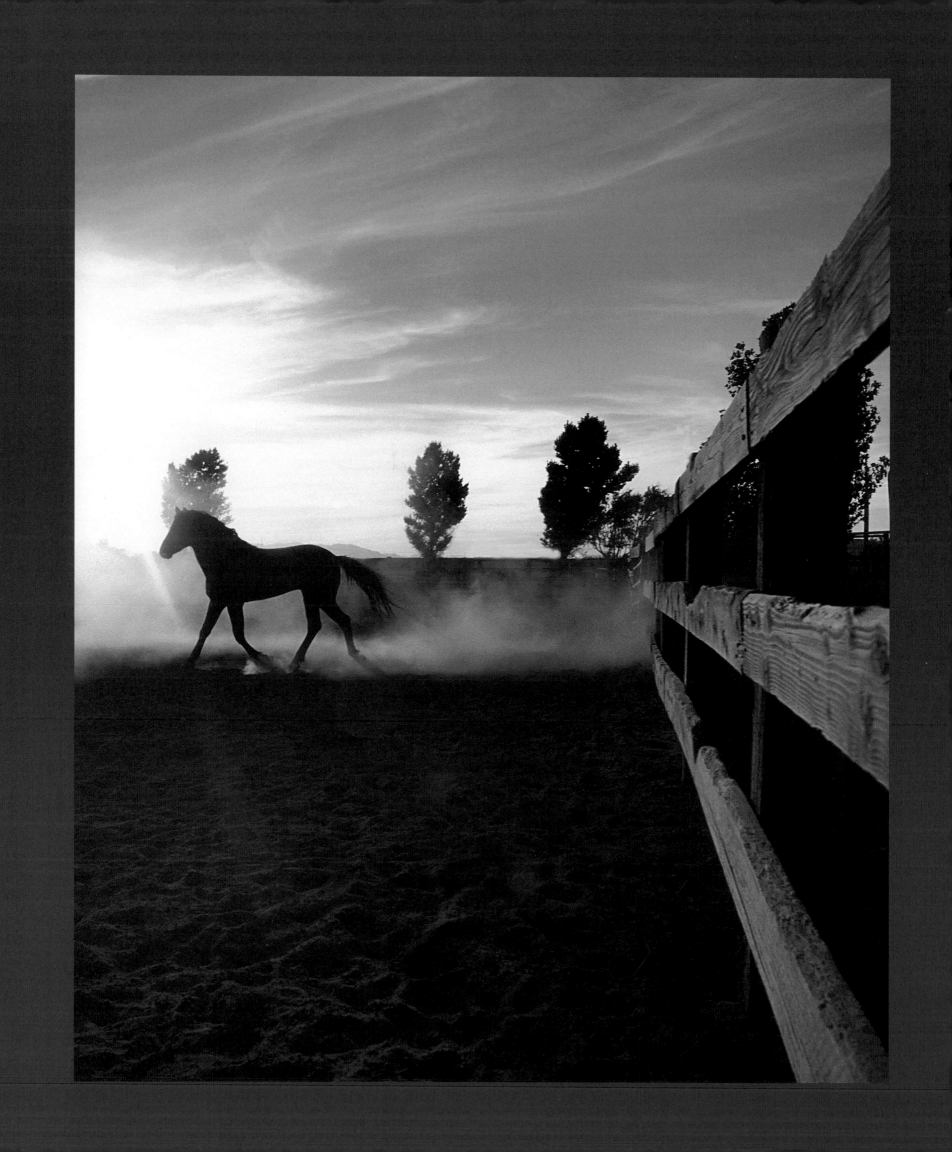

To join together with other creatures in a song of joy moves us to experience the sacred in even the most mundane phenomena, transporting us from a self-centered way of being into a state in which we embrace, and are embraced by, all and everything.

— ADELE, DEBORAH, AND THOMAS McCORMICK, *Horses and the Mystical Path*

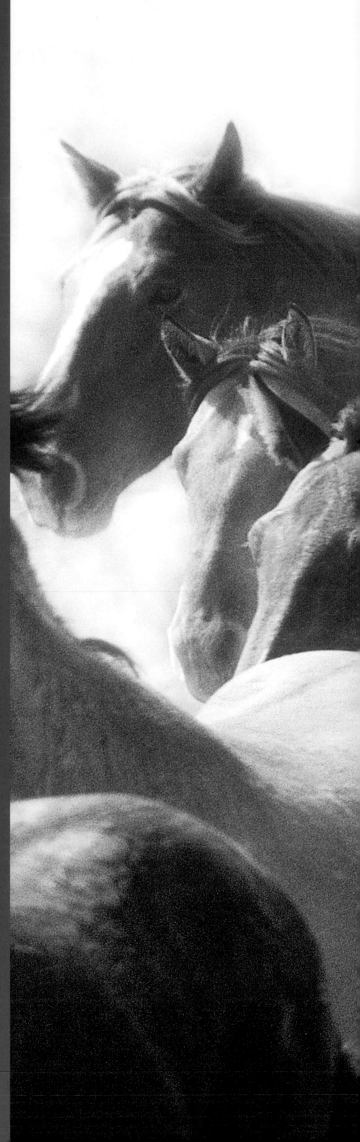

We need another and a wiser and perhaps a
more mystical concept of animals. Remote from
universal nature, and living by complicated
artifice, man in civilization surveys the creature
through the glass of his knowledge and sees
thereby a feather magnified and the whole image
in distortion. We patronize them for their
incompleteness, for their tragic fate of having
taken form so far below ourselves. And therein
we err, and greatly err. For the animal shall not
be measured by man. In a world more complete
than ours, they move finished and complete,
gifted with extensions of the senses we have lost
or never attained, living by voices we shall never
hear. They are not underlings; they are other
nations, caught with ourselves in the net of life
and time, fellow prisoners of the splendor and
travail of earth.

— HENRY BESTON,
The Outermost House

The worst sin towards our fellow creatures is not to hate them, but to be indifferent to them. That's the essence of inhumanity.

— GEORGE BERNARD SHAW

Different forms of life in different aspects of existence make up the teeming denizens of this earth of ours . . . and all beings primarily seek peace, comfort, and security. Life is as dear to a mute creature as it is to a man. Just as one wants happiness and fears pain, just as one wants to live and not to die, so do other creatures.

— HIS HOLINESS THE DALAI LAMA

Living and working with horses expands
our awareness of Creation and allows us to
experience and enjoy a new dimension of
intimacy with it.

— ADELE, DEBORAH, AND
THOMAS McCORMICK,
Horses and the Mystical Path

In my path, through my constant search, my horse has taught me the limitless progression of life. Every time in my learning that I felt a breakthrough, I opened the doors and I found my horse saying, "It's about time. I've been waiting for you." A few weeks later another breakthrough. I opened the doors and there was my horse again. So far I have never found any limits but my own.

— DOMINIQUE BARBIER

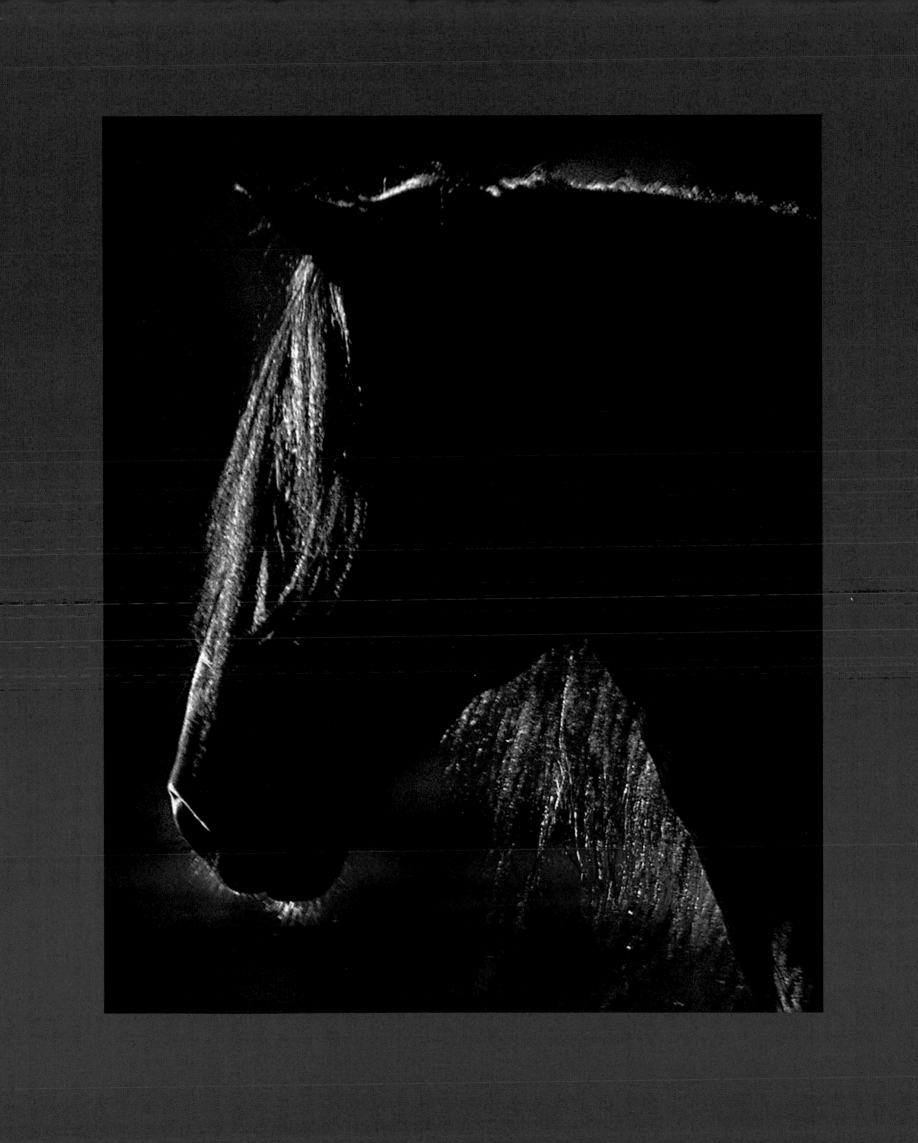

Every animal is a gateway to the phenomenal world of the human spirit. What most fail to realize is that what they think of animals reflects the way they think of themselves.

— TED ANDREWS, *Animal-Speak*

We act in our own best interests when we...let [horses] guide us, because in the eyes of these reflective, openhearted creatures, we can never be too joyful, too beautiful — or too free.

— LINDA KOHANOV,
Riding between the Worlds

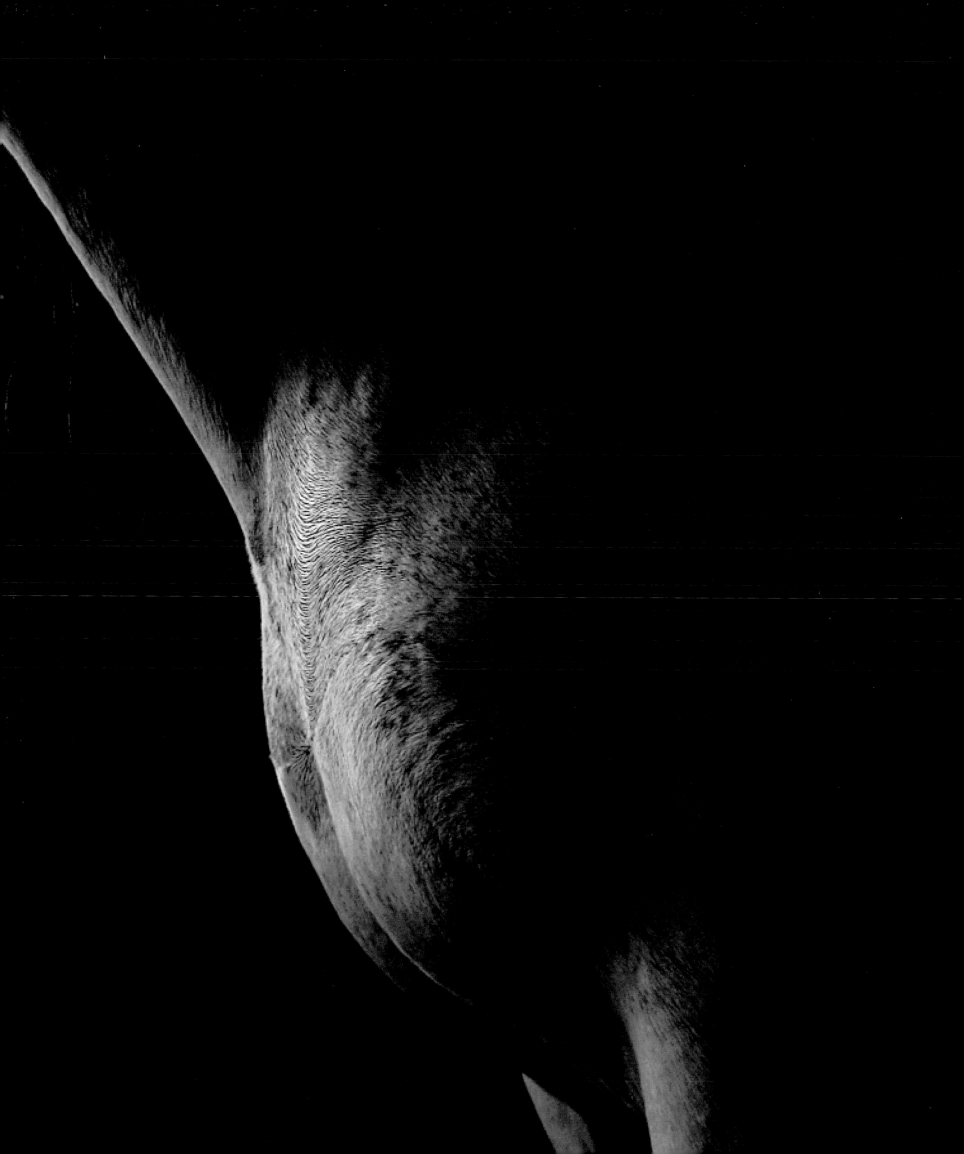

Far back, far back in our dark soul, the horse prances.

— D. H. LAWRENCE

The eternal being, as it lives in us, also lives in every animal.

— ARTHUR SCHOPENHAUER

I was born upon the prairie, where the wind blew free, and there was nothing to break the light of the sun. I was born where there were no enclosures, and where everything drew a free breath.. I lived like my fathers before me, and like them, I lived happily.

— TEN BEARS, YAMPARIKA COMANCHE CHIEF

Until he extends his circle of compassion to include all living things man himself will not find peace.

— ALBERT SCHWEITZER

Horses are fiercely loyal and committed. They give us tremendous gifts, if we only allow ourselves to be open to them.

— KATE SOLISTI-MATTELON,
Conversations with Horse

Horse and human travel as partners, ever cognizant that wherever humanity has left its footprint in the long ascent from barbarism to civilization, there is the hoofprint of the horse beside it.

— DR. SHERRY ACKERMAN,
Dressage in the Fourth Dimension

The elders were wise. They knew that man's heart, away from nature, becomes hard; they knew that lack of respect for growing, living things, soon led to lack of respect for humans, too.

— CHIEF LUTHER STANDING BEAR,
LAKOTA SIOUX

Learning about our horses is learning about ourselves.

— LINDA TELLINGTON-JONES

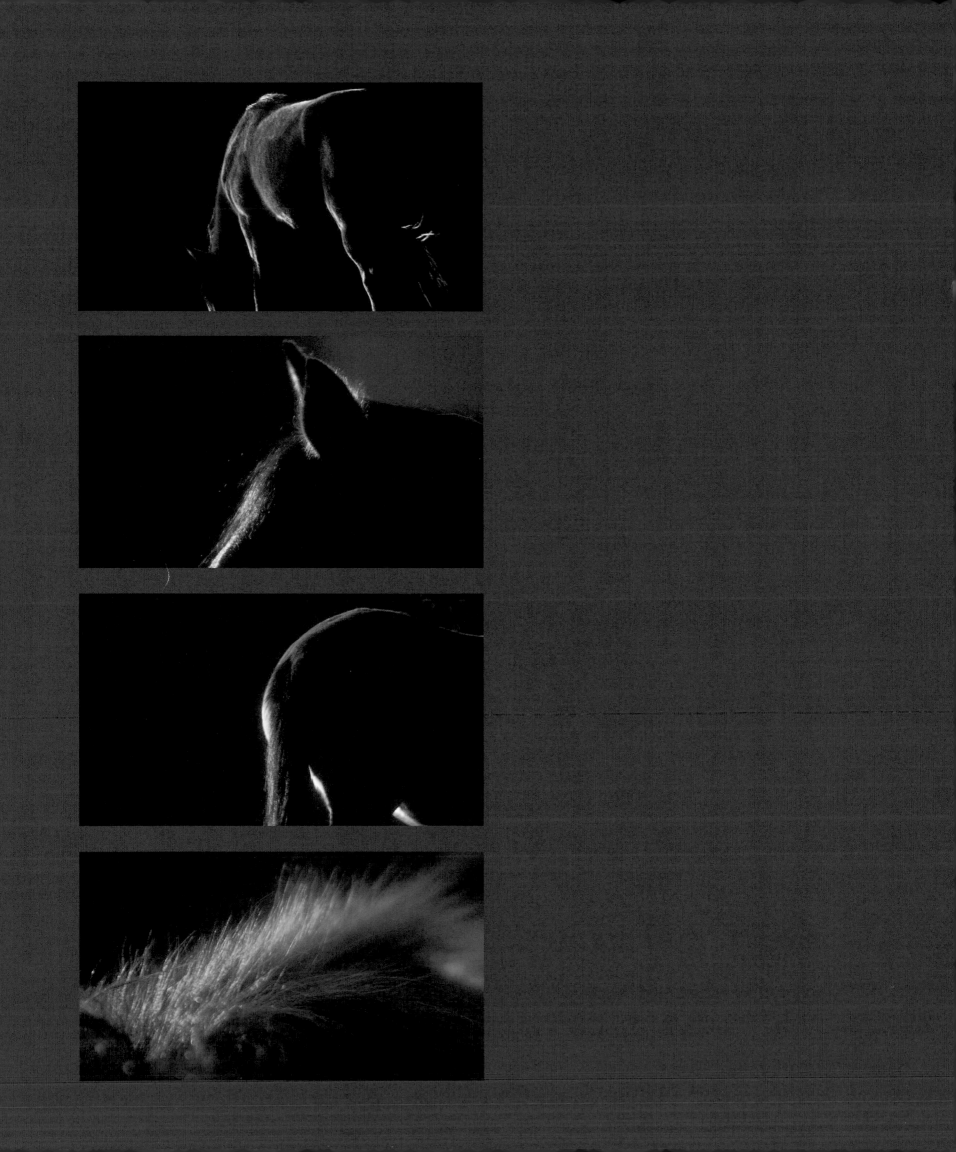

If you want to get close to the horse, you have to get close to yourself. Then the horse can come to you.

— CAROL NICHOLS

Horses are persistently hopeful that humanity will wake up.

— KATE SOLISTI-MATTELON,
Conversations with Horse

If you talk to the animals they will talk with you and you will know each other. If you do not talk to them you will not know them and what you do not know, you will fear. What one fears, one destroys.

— CHIEF DAN GEORGE

In their innocence and wisdom, in their connection to the
earth and its most ancient rhythms, animals show us a way
back to a home they have never left.

— SUSAN CHERNAK McELROY,
Animals as Teachers and Healers

Love of animals is a universal impulse, a
common ground on which all of us may meet.
By loving and understanding animals, perhaps
we as humans shall come to understand each
other.

— DR. LOUIS J. CAMUTI

New World Library is dedicated to publishing books and other media that inspire and challenge us to improve the quality of our lives and the world.

We are a socially and environmentally aware company and we make every attempt to embody the ideals presented in our publications. We recognize that we have an ethical responsibility to our customers, our employees, and our planet. We serve our customers by creating the finest publications possible on personal growth, creativity, fulfillment, and other areas of emerging importance. We serve our employees with generous benefits, significant profit sharing, and constant encouragement to pursue our most expansive dreams.

As members of the Green Press Initiative, we print an increasing number of books with soy-based ink on 100% postconsumer waste recycled paper. We also power our offices with solar energy and contribute to nonprofit organizations working to make the world a better place for us all.

Our products are available in bookstores everywhere.
For our catalog, please contact:

New World Library
14 Pamaron Way
Novato, California 94949

Phone: (415) 884-2100 or (800) 972-6657
Catalog requests: Ext. 50
Orders: Ext. 52
Fax: (415) 884-2199

Email: escort@newworldlibrary.com
Website: www.newworldlibrary.com